Ft. Lauderdale

GAYCATION

William Giancursio

Ft. Lauderdale
GAYCATION

On the morning of February 22, 2008, I woke up excited to see cold, blustery snow drifts on my front lawn. In a few short hours I would be basking in the tropical Florida sun, leisurely sipping cocktails by the pool at a guest house in Ft. Lauderdale. By mid-afternoon, I would either be napping or be bored out of my mind. I do enjoy the feel of the hot sun, especially during a dreary northern winter. It's just that I don't like to lay in the sun and fry. I usually bring a sketch book with me and sit in the shade and draw.

Uncertain of my intentions, I walked into my art studio and began pulling together some drawing supplies. I needed to be at the Rochester airport within a half hour, and I was still deciding what to bring. As I glanced around the room, I was surrounded by the sets and props from my previous book, HARD, as well as a cast of about 20 clothed and nude action figures. Do I dare take some of them with me? Without pre-constructed sets, what would I do once I got them there? Excited by the spontaneity of the moment and the shortage of time, I began gathering up toys, props and outfits suitable for a 10-day visit to Ft Lauderdale. Although barely finished packing myself, I had begun to coordinate outfits for "the boys." I was packing bags for my action figures! Somebody needed to call my therapist. Thus began the inspiration and the madness for this book, my third in the gay-play series.

On the airplane, I thought about how to approach the difference in scale between "the boys" and the real world. In the first group of photographs I took they appeared to be dwarfed by their surroundings. I contemplated playing with this illusion, but to my surprise, in one of the shots, they actually appeared to be life-size in relationship to everything else. What a moment divine! My muse was formulated, my motivation defined. I would explore the optical illusion of scale and space.

All of the photographs of "the boys" were taken holding them at arms length from the lens of the camera. I used a maximum depth of field setting. None of the illusions were created with any computer-assisted programs. The photographs were all taken in real time in actual places all around Ft Lauderdale. Most of the people around me ignored what I was doing. This was a blessing in disguise as the dignity lost while conversing with "the boys", during shooting, can never be restored.

On a final note, we live in a world of text-messaging and chat rooms. In this cyber-world of condensed gratification, new words and ideas are coined every minute. Evolving thoughts take on a new significance at the punch of a keypad or the whim of our imagination. Vacations have morphed into daycations and staycations. We have even combined and abbreviated the names of sportsmen and celebrities.

In keeping with the spirit of the times, I would like to welcome you to join me in a place where fantasy and reality merge. A place where toys will be boys and truth is just a well-framed illusion. I call this ideal place a gaycation.

William Giancursio

for
Tom

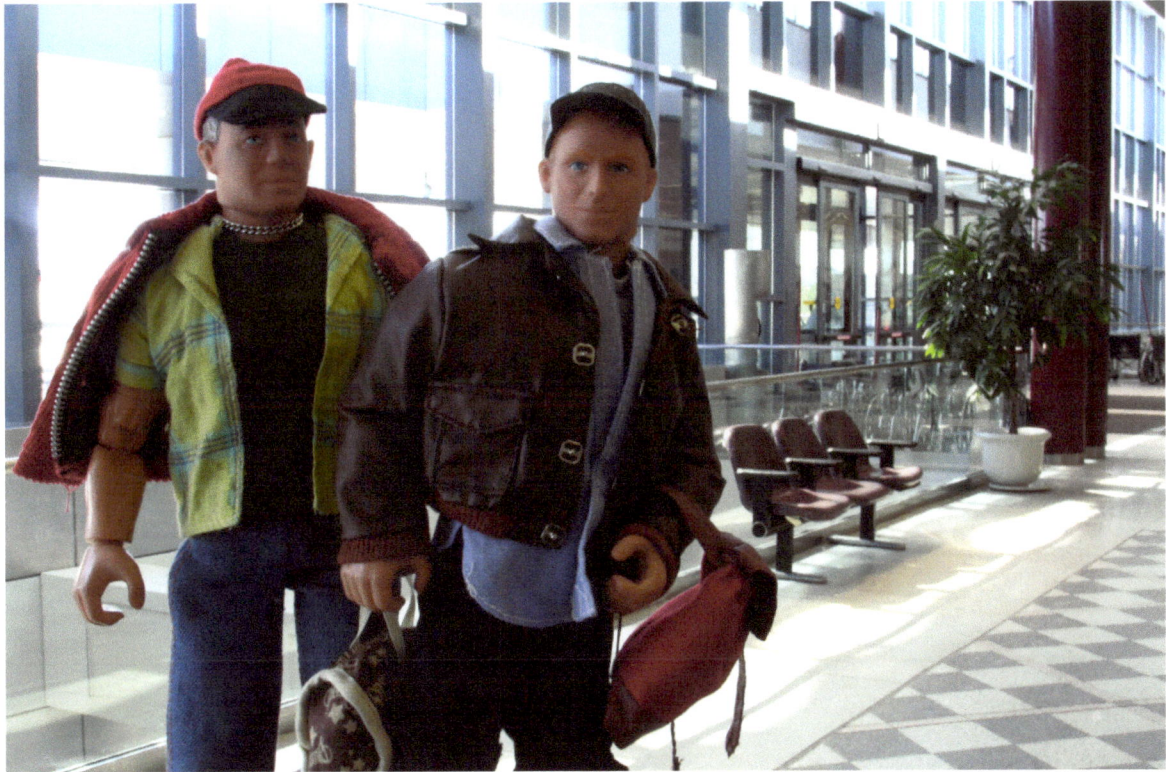

8 F

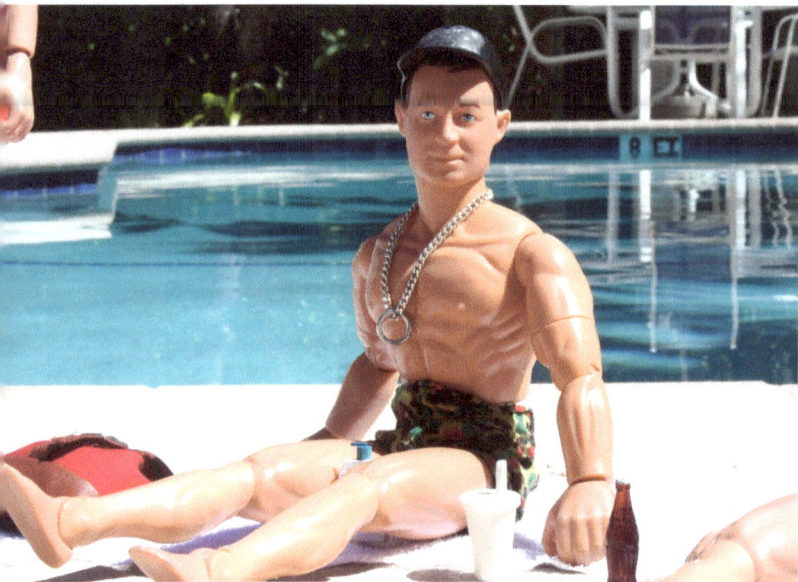

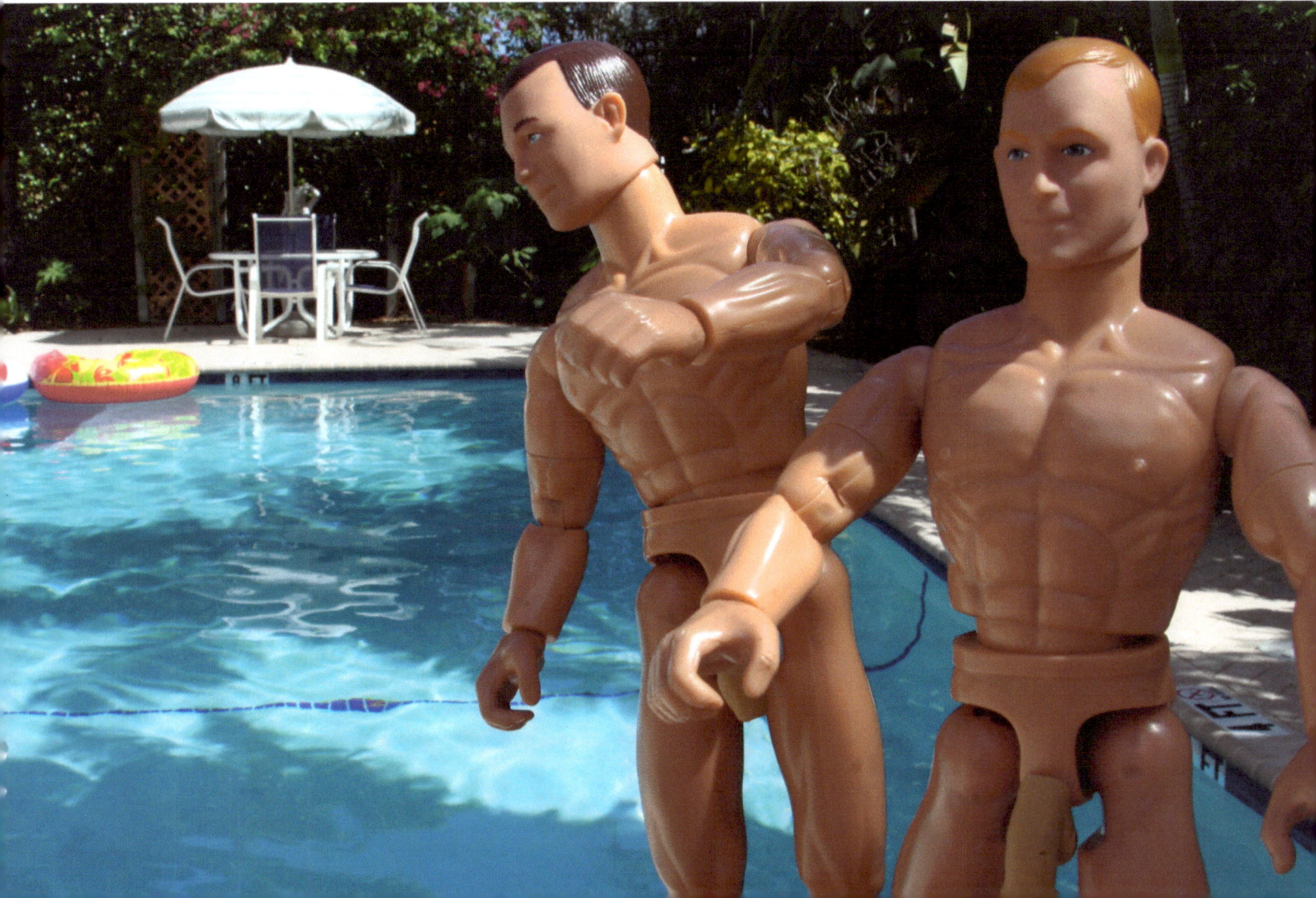

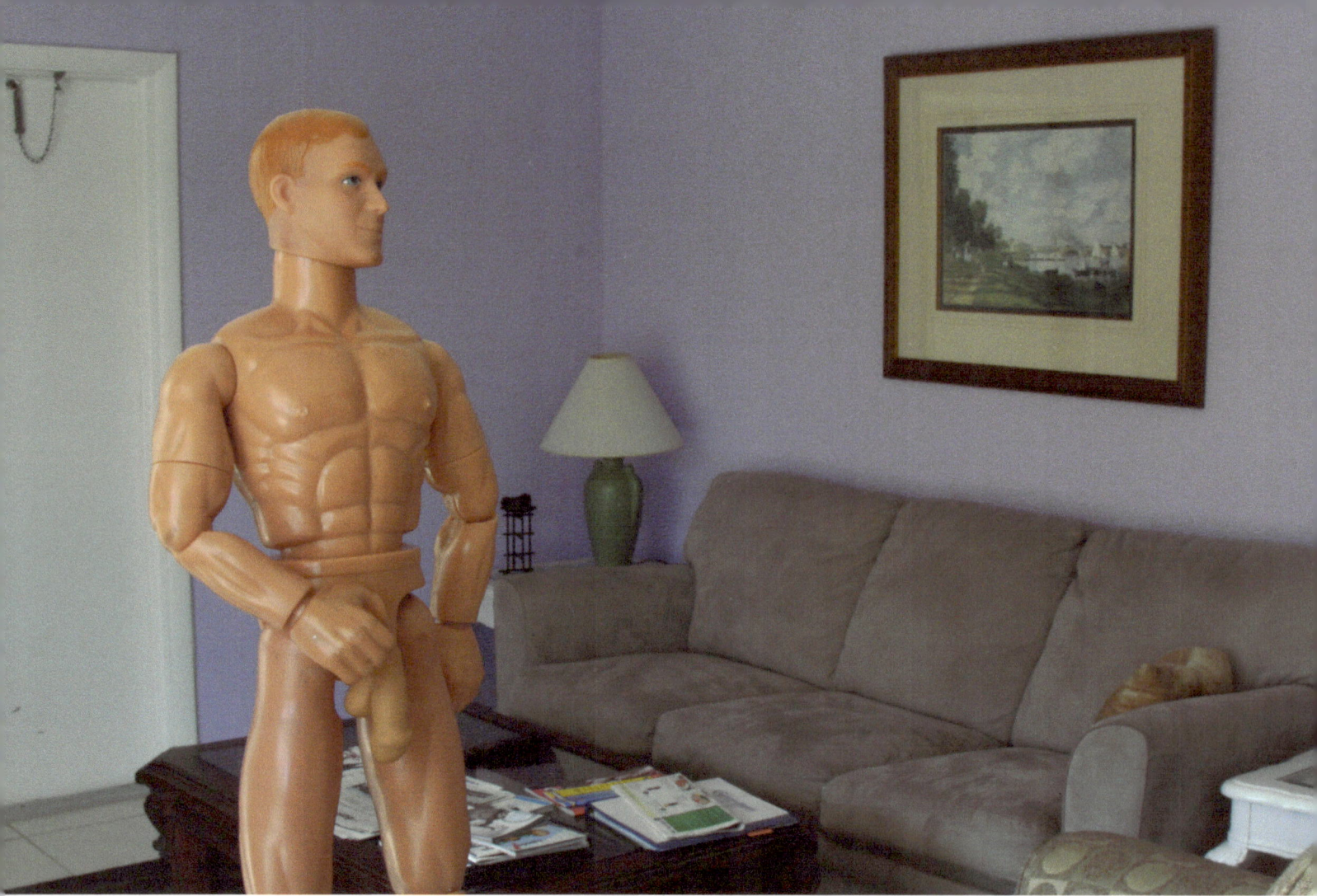

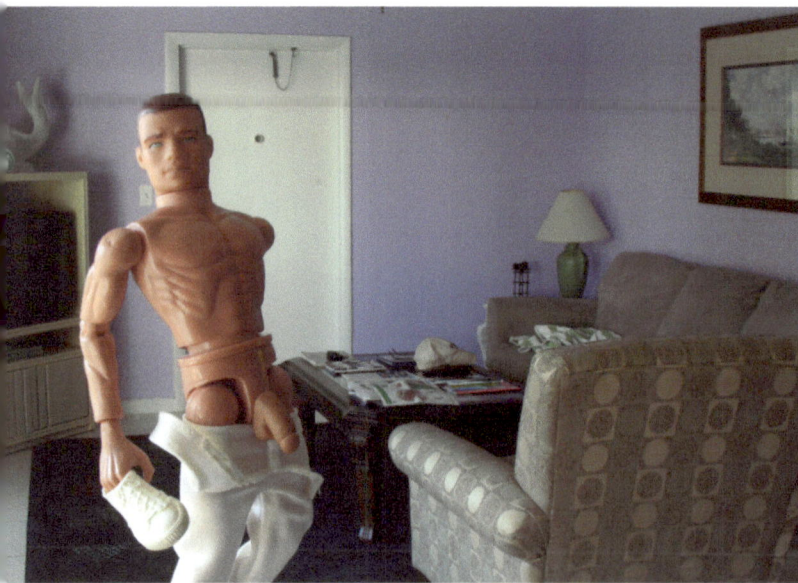

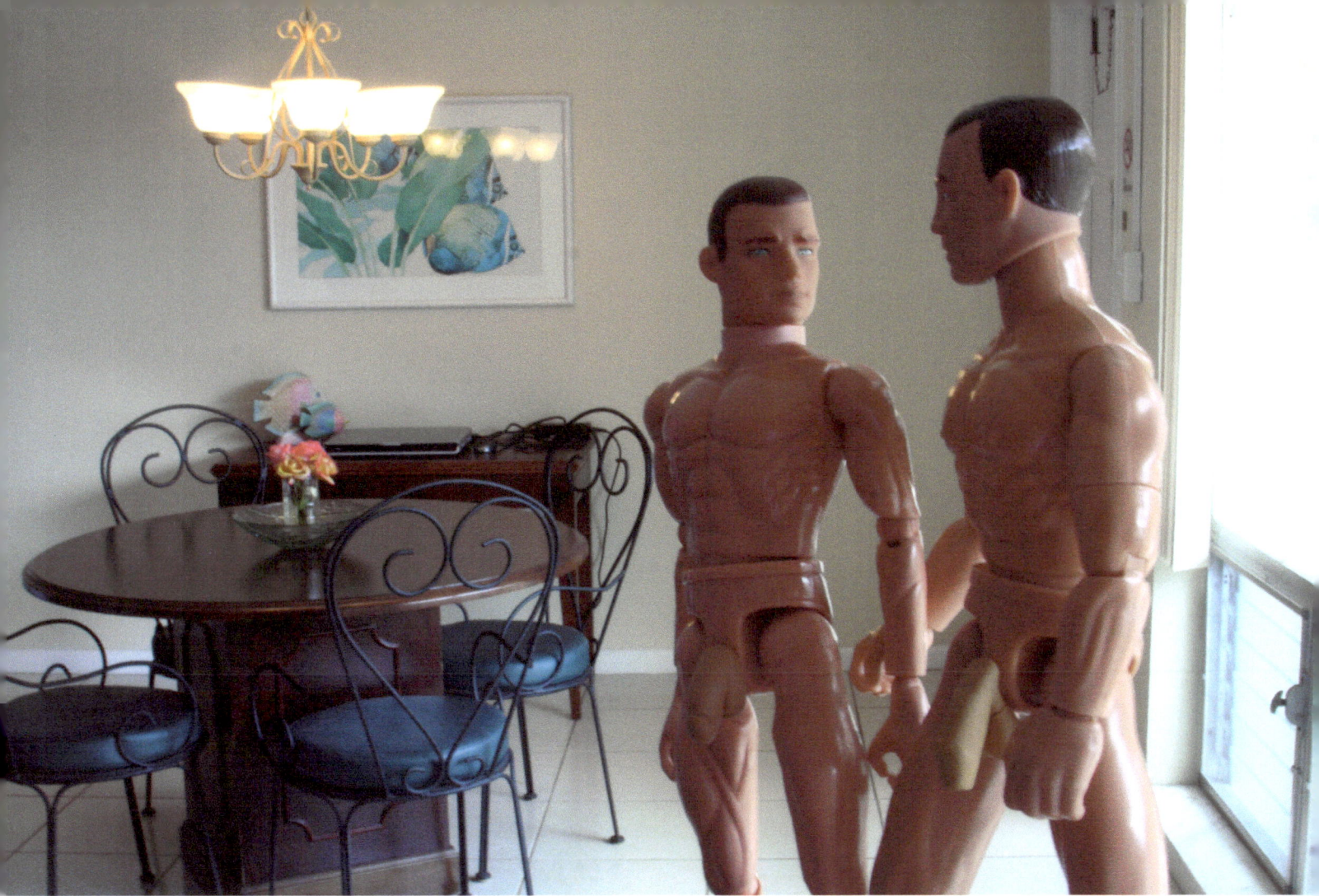

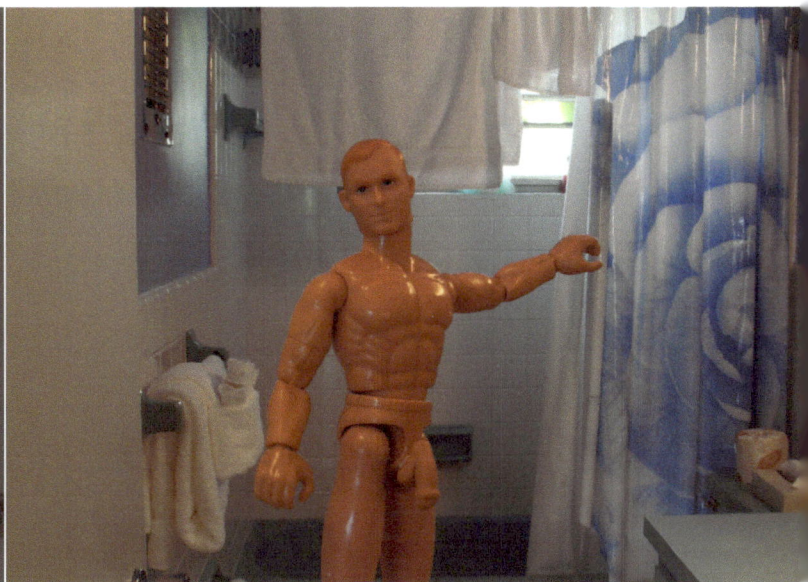

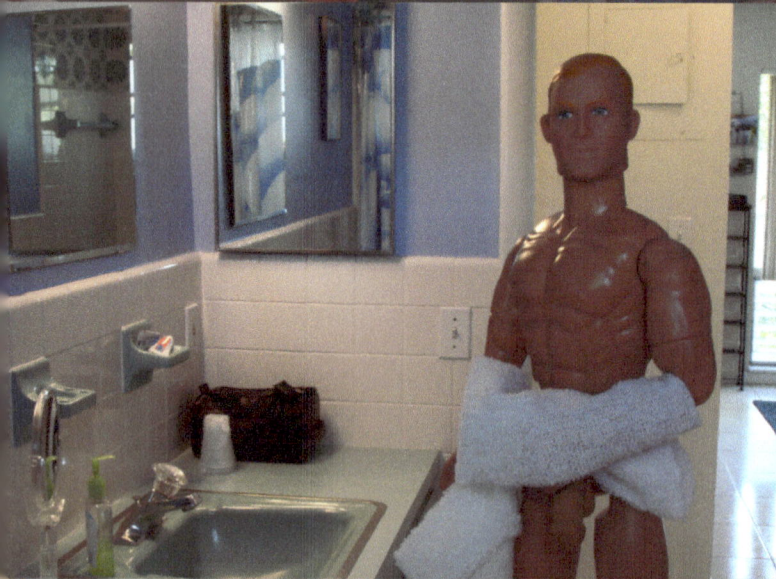

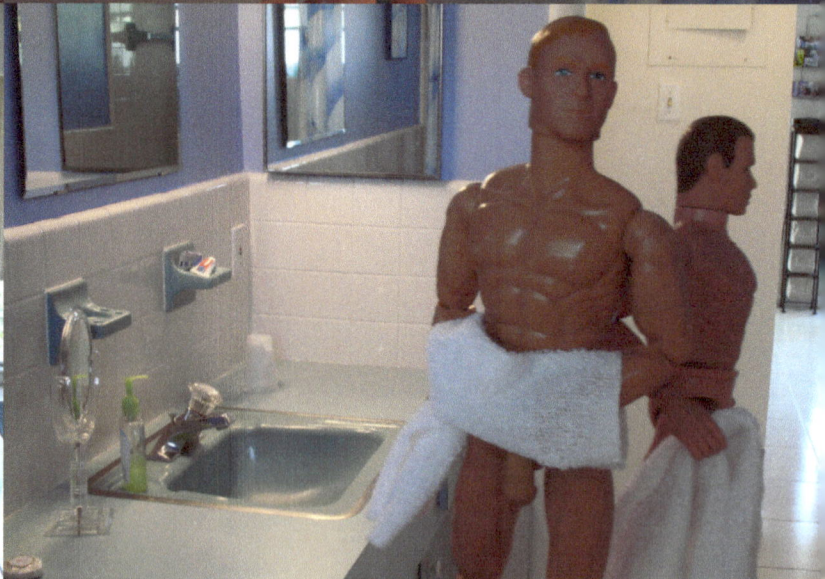

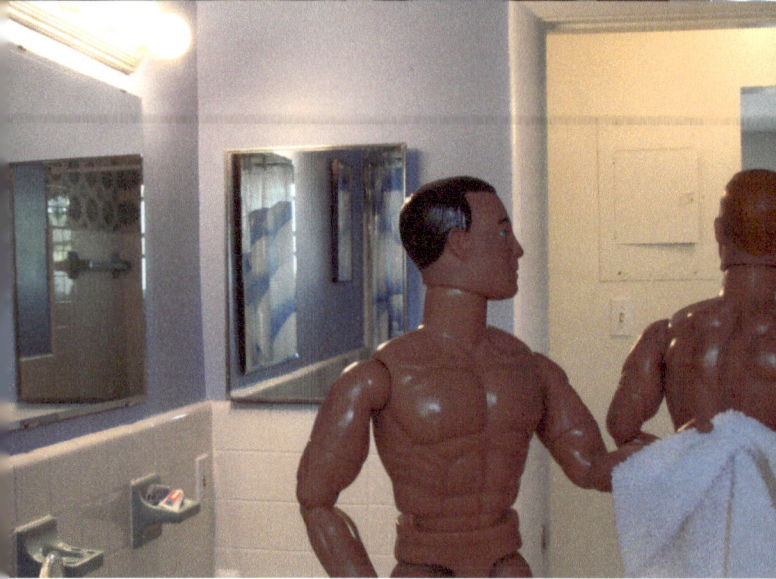

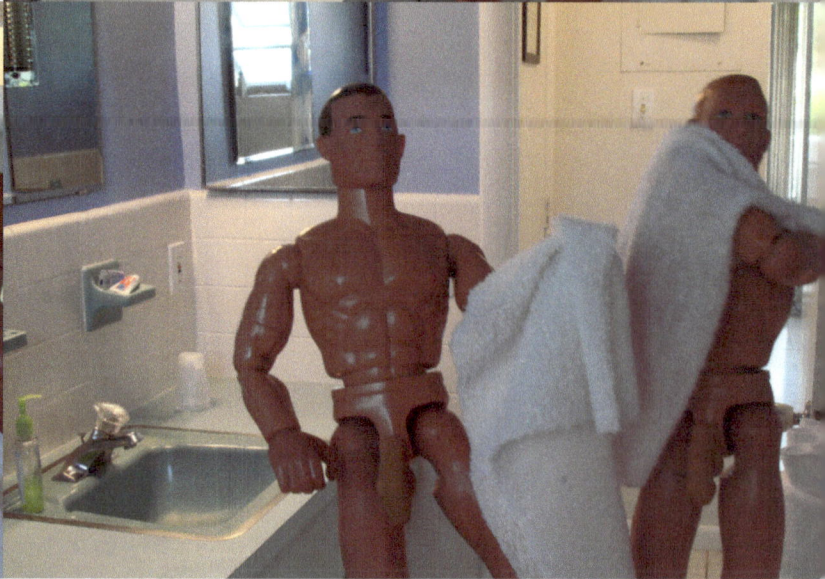

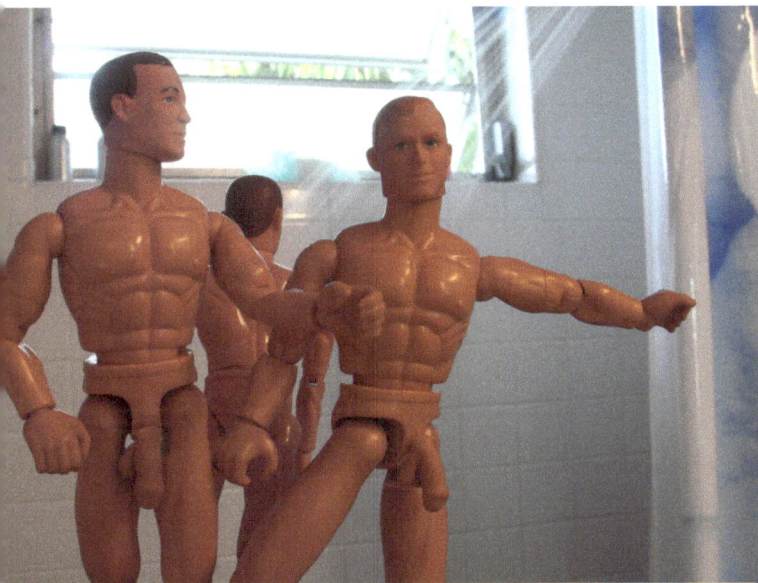

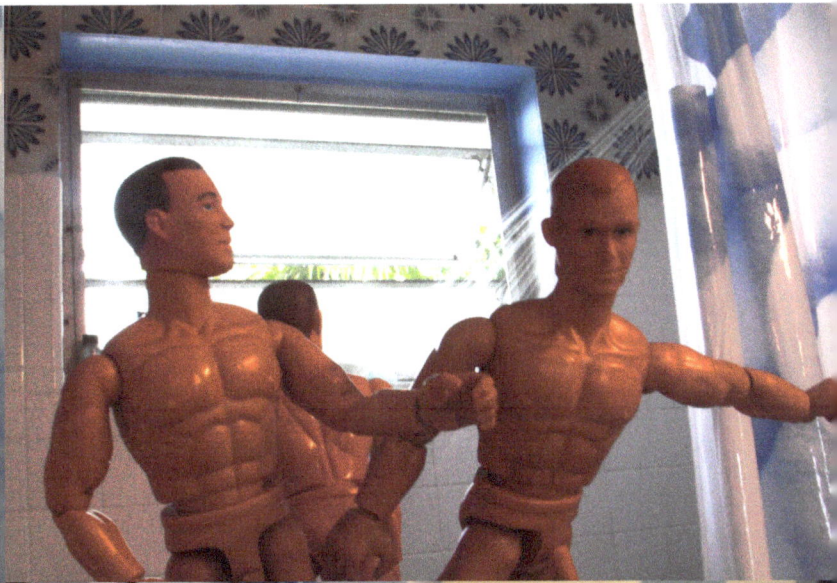

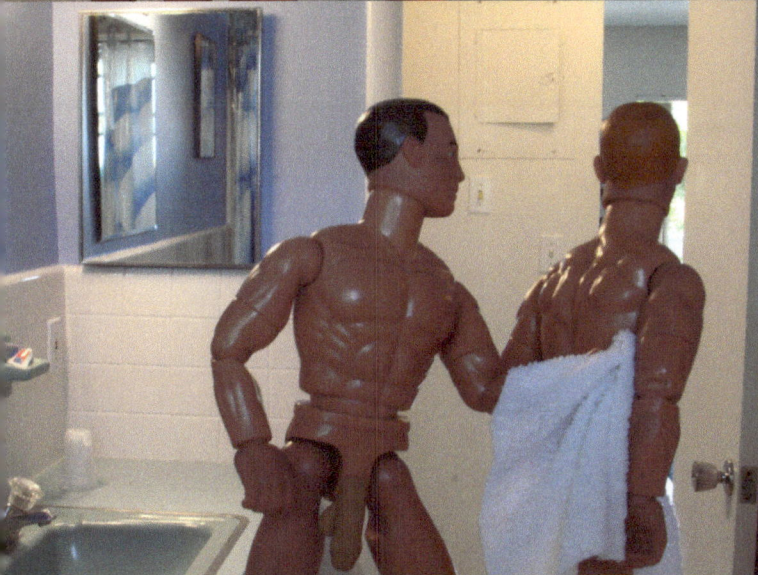

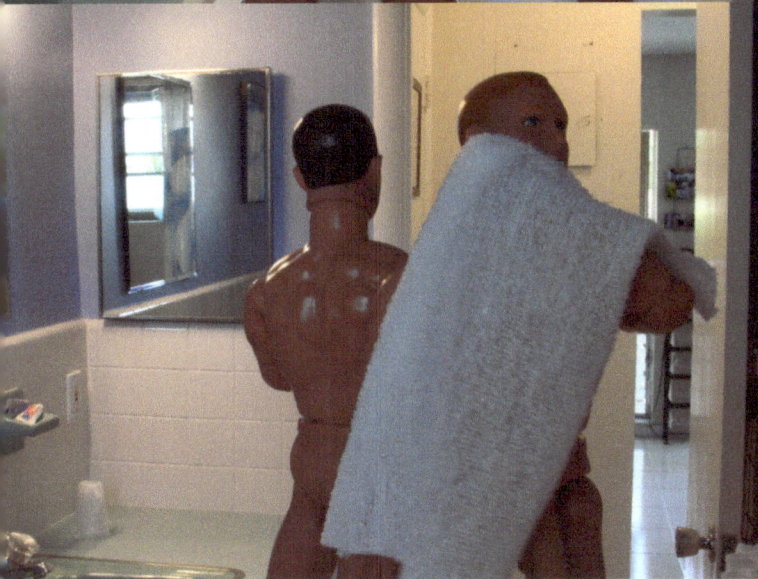

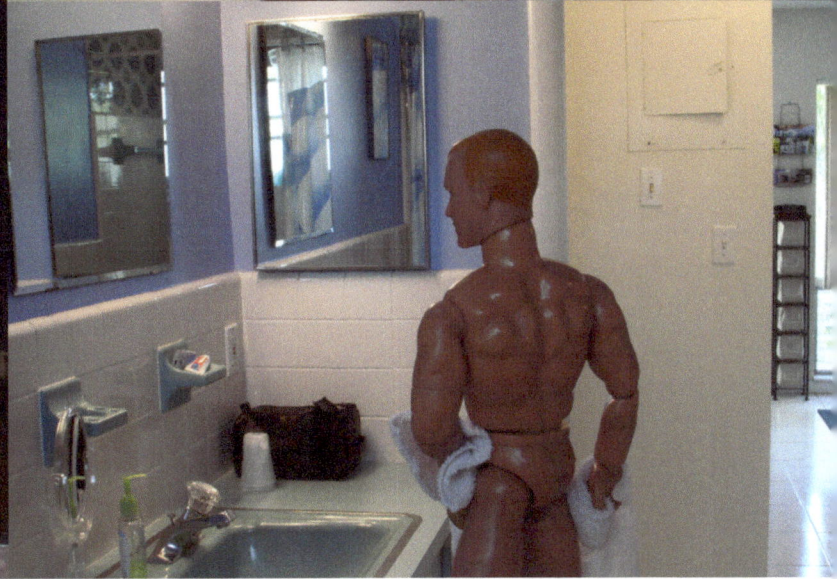

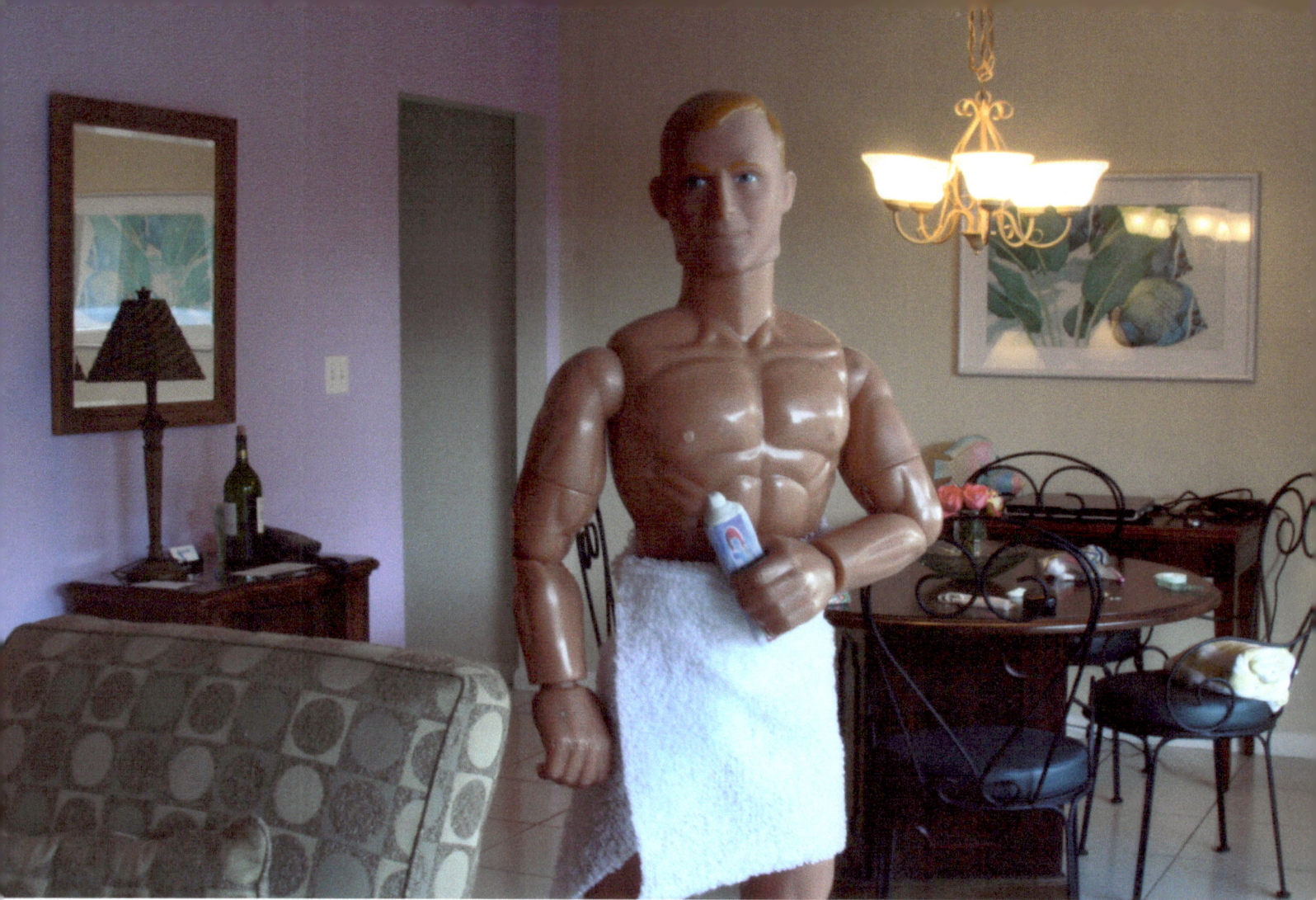

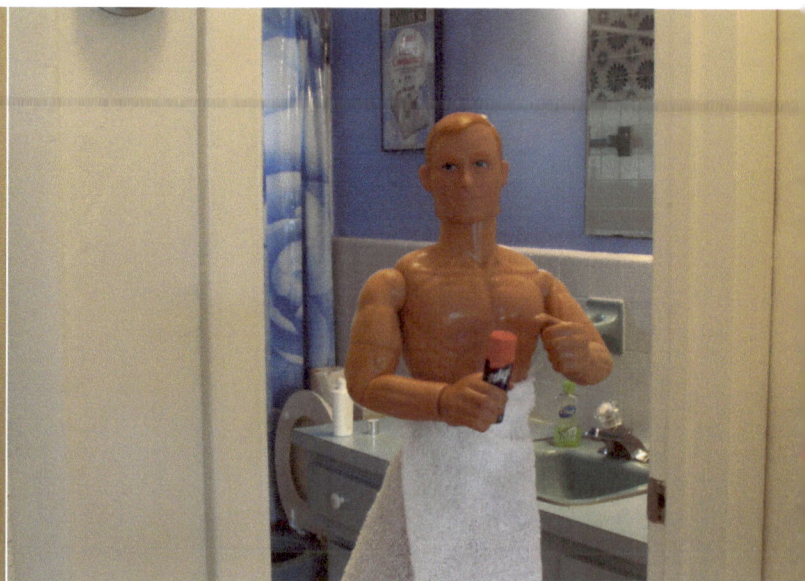

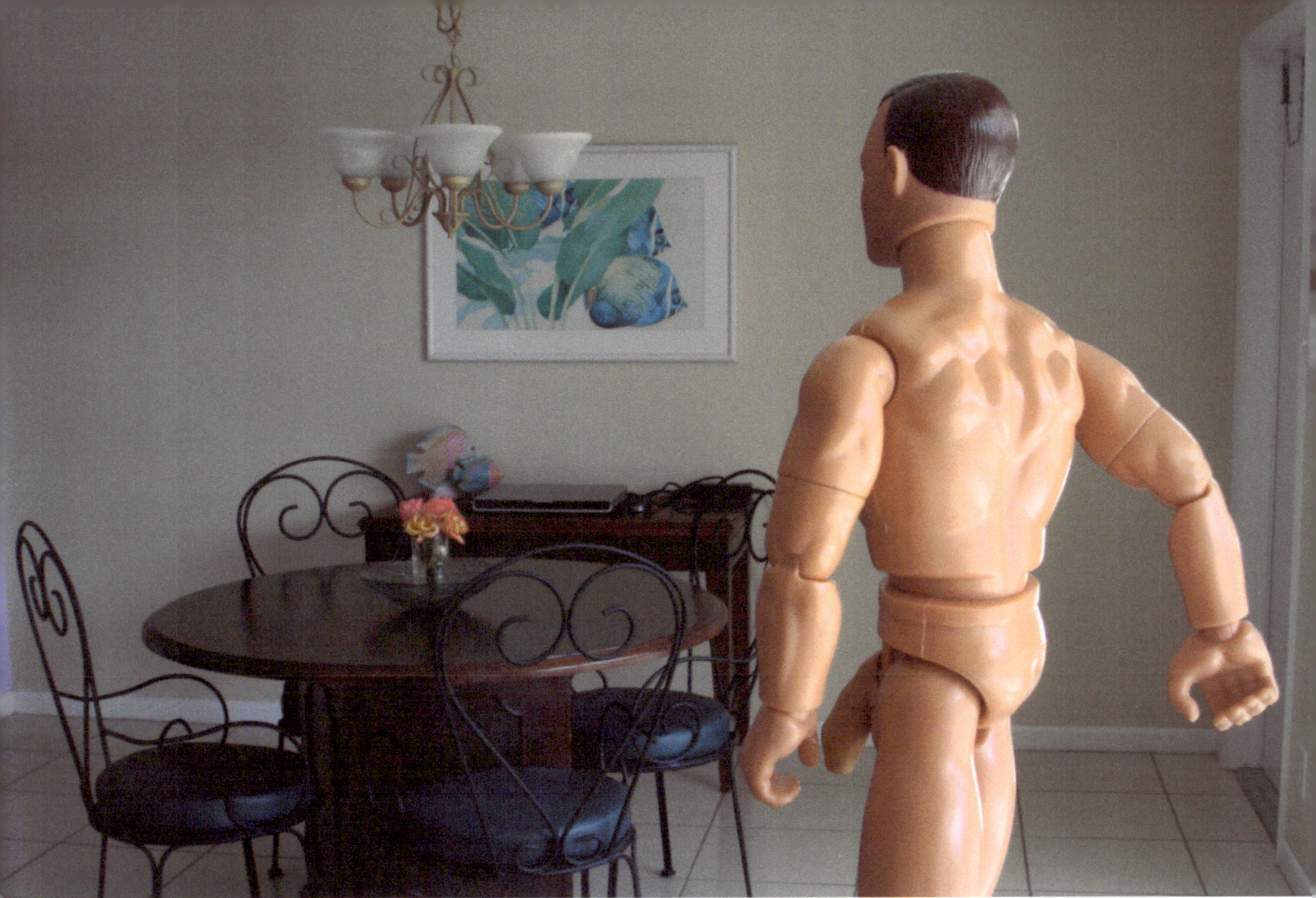

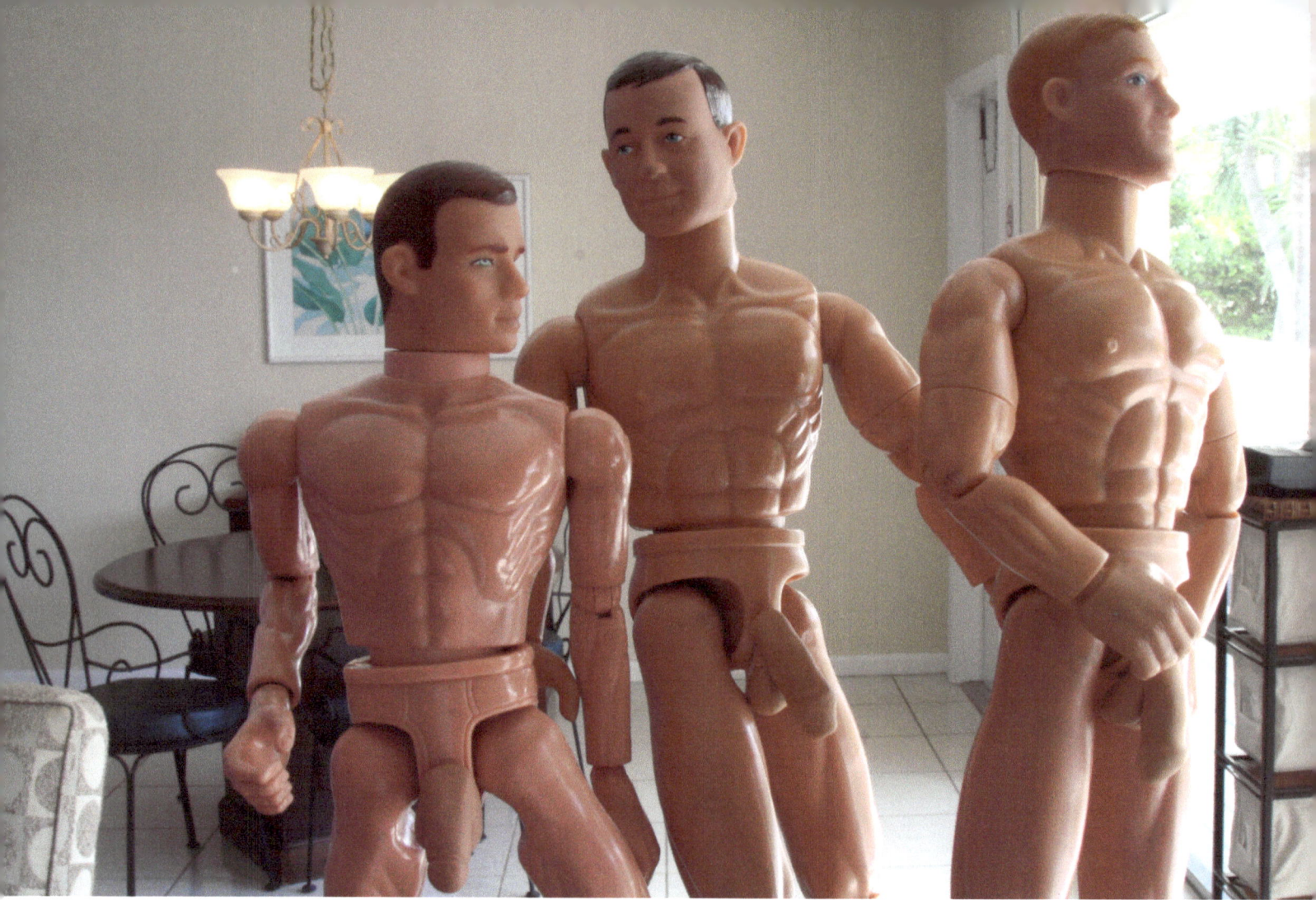

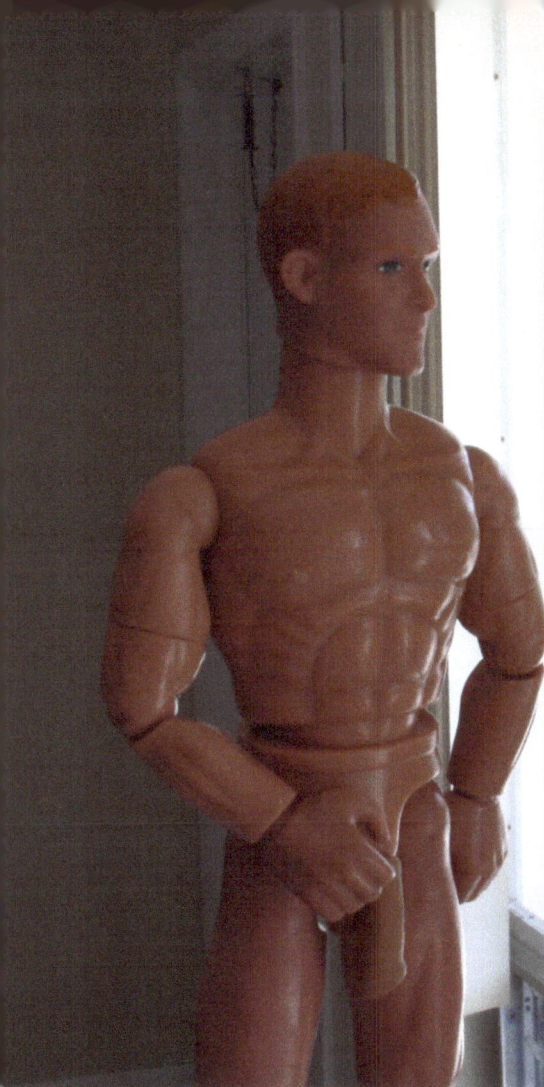

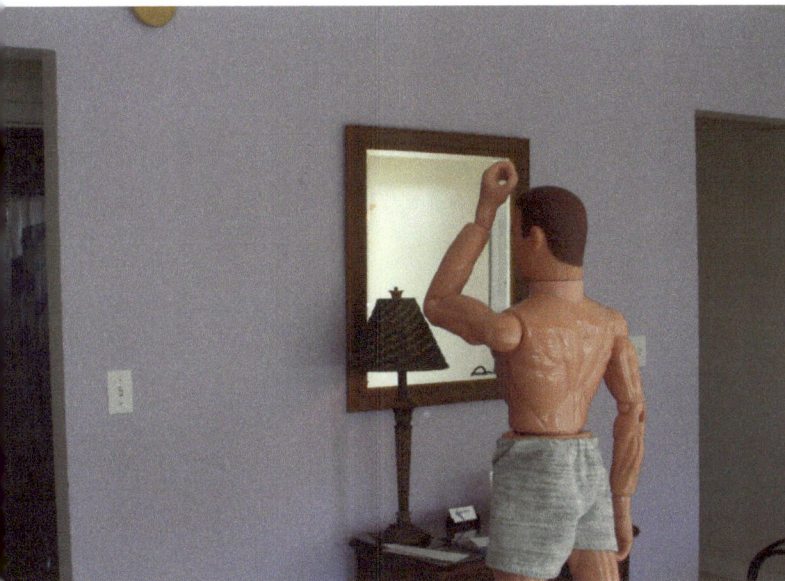

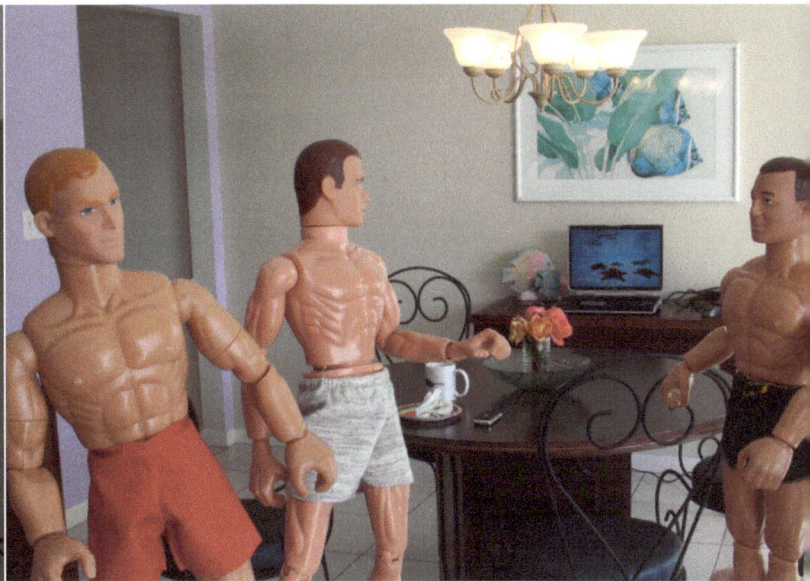

341
The Fort Lauderdale
YACHT & BEACH CLUB

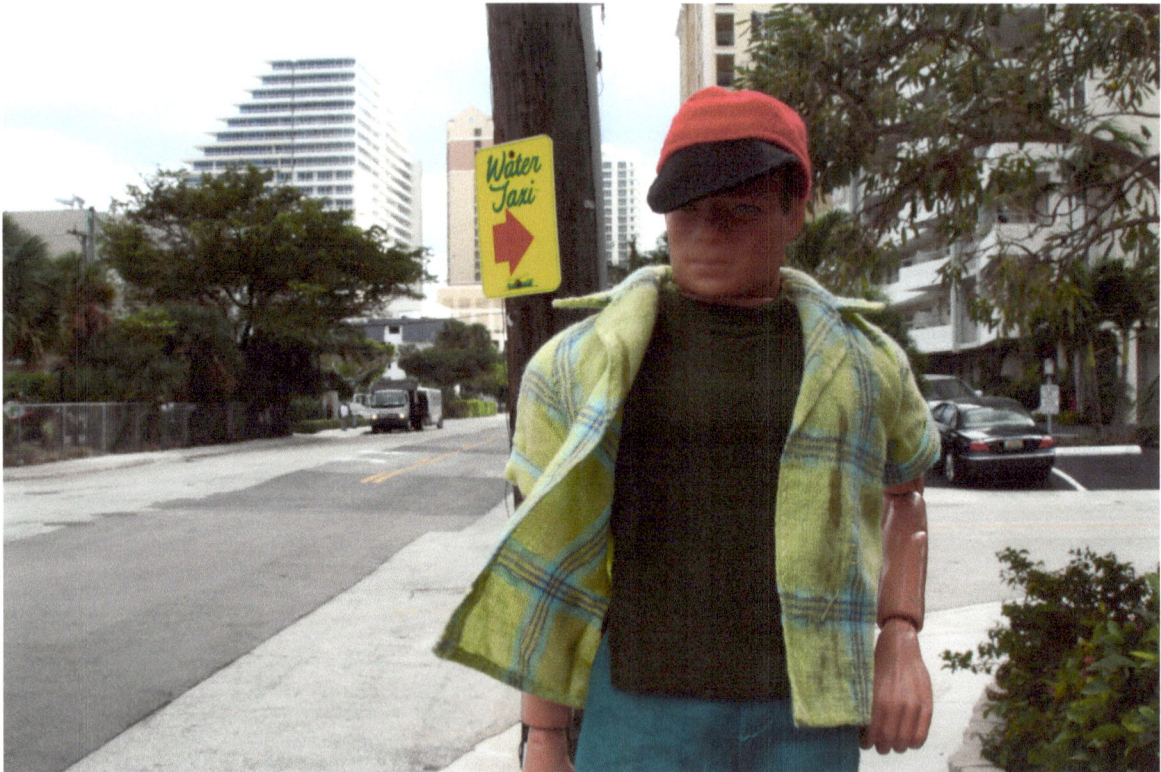

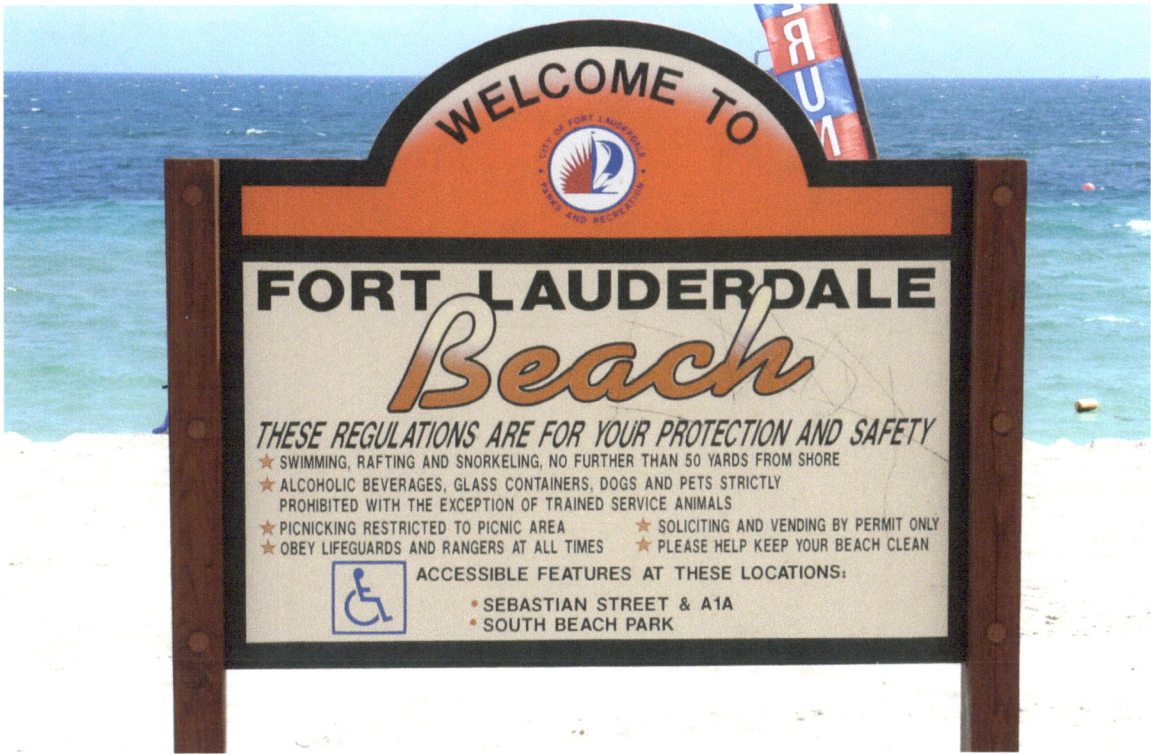

WELCOME TO

FORT LAUDERDALE
Beach

THESE REGULATIONS ARE FOR YOUR PROTECTION AND SAFETY

★ SWIMMING, RAFTING AND SNORKELING, NO FURTHER THAN 50 YARDS FROM SHORE
★ ALCOHOLIC BEVERAGES, GLASS CONTAINERS, DOGS AND PETS STRICTLY
   PROHIBITED WITH THE EXCEPTION OF TRAINED SERVICE ANIMALS
★ PICNICKING RESTRICTED TO PICNIC AREA   ★ SOLICITING AND VENDING BY PERMIT ONLY
★ OBEY LIFEGUARDS AND RANGERS AT ALL TIMES ★ PLEASE HELP KEEP YOUR BEACH CLEAN

ACCESSIBLE FEATURES AT THESE LOCATIONS:

• SEBASTIAN STREET & A1A
• SOUTH BEACH PARK

SEBASTIAN ST

SEBASTIAN

BUS STOP

40

WELCOME TO
FORT LAUDERDALE
Beach
THESE REGULATIONS ARE FOR YOUR PROTECTION AND SAFETY

YAMAHA

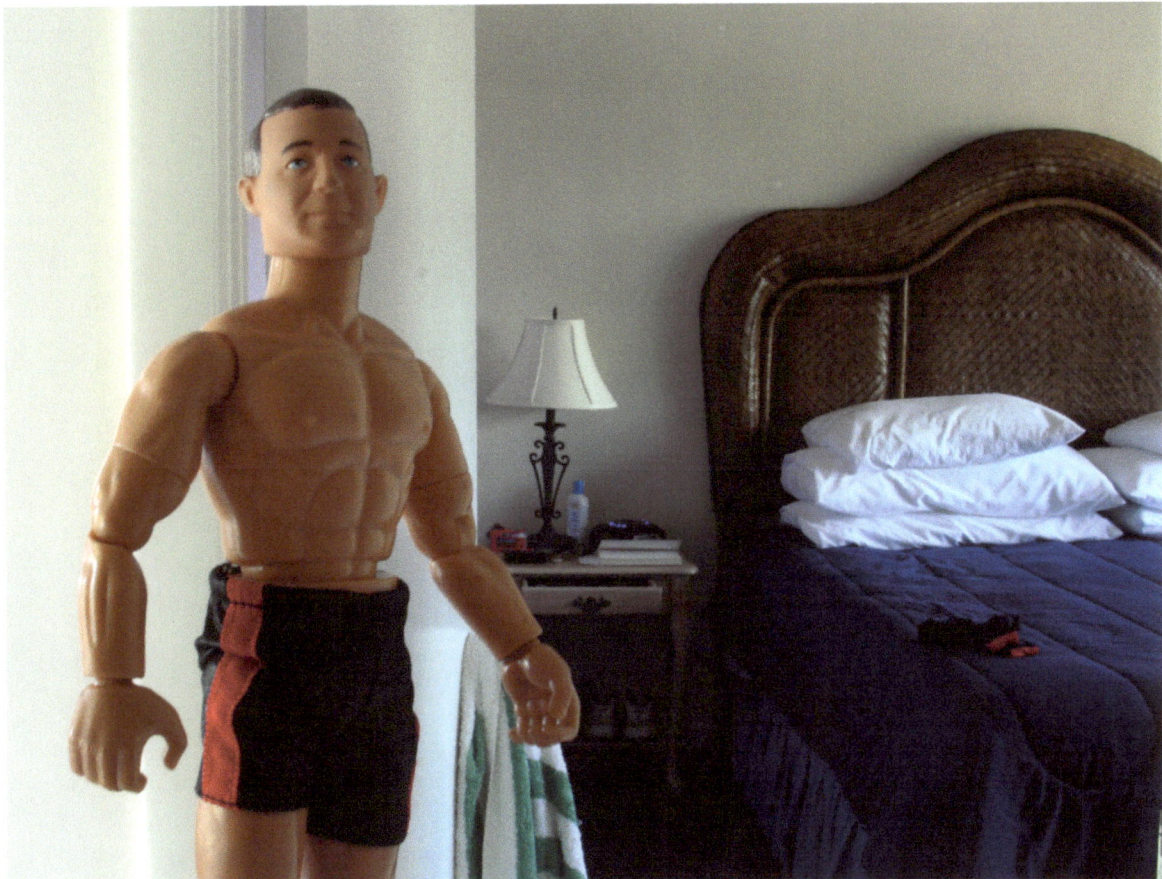

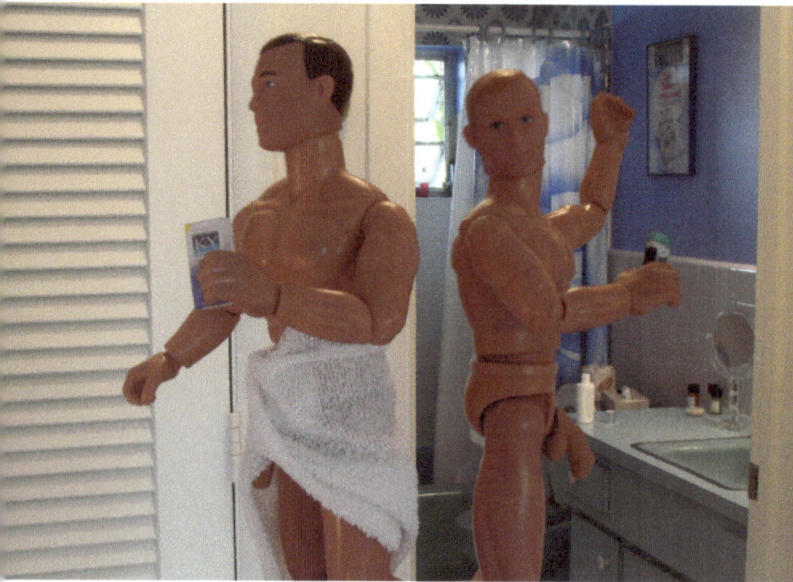

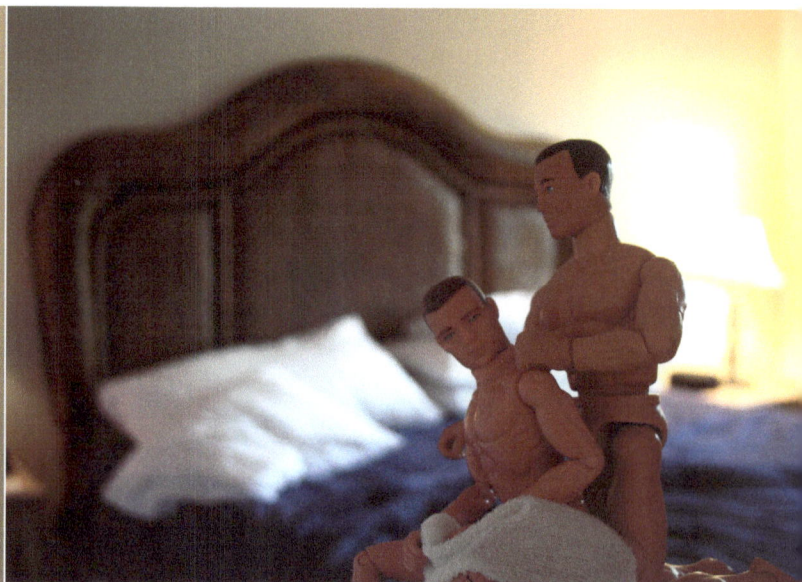

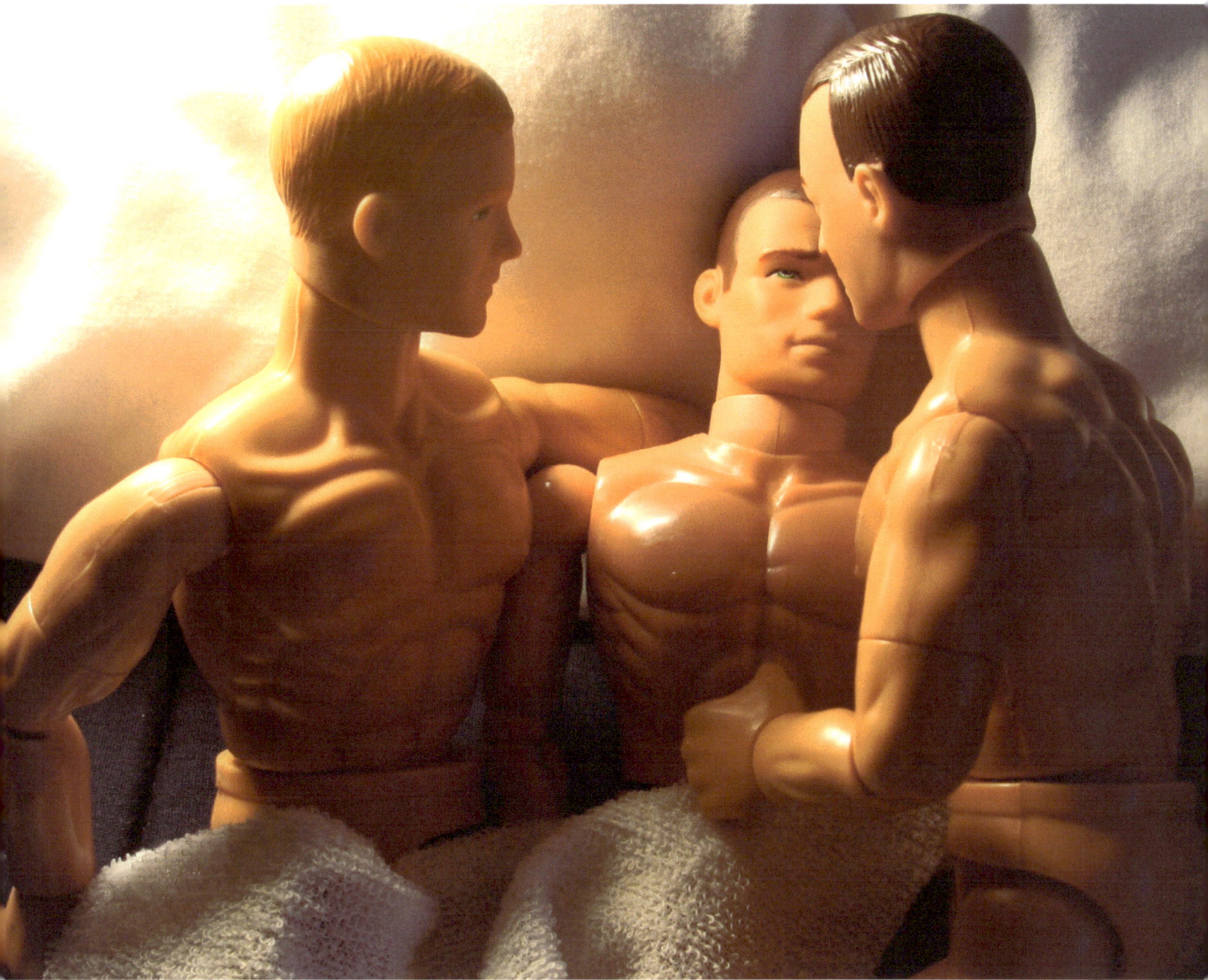

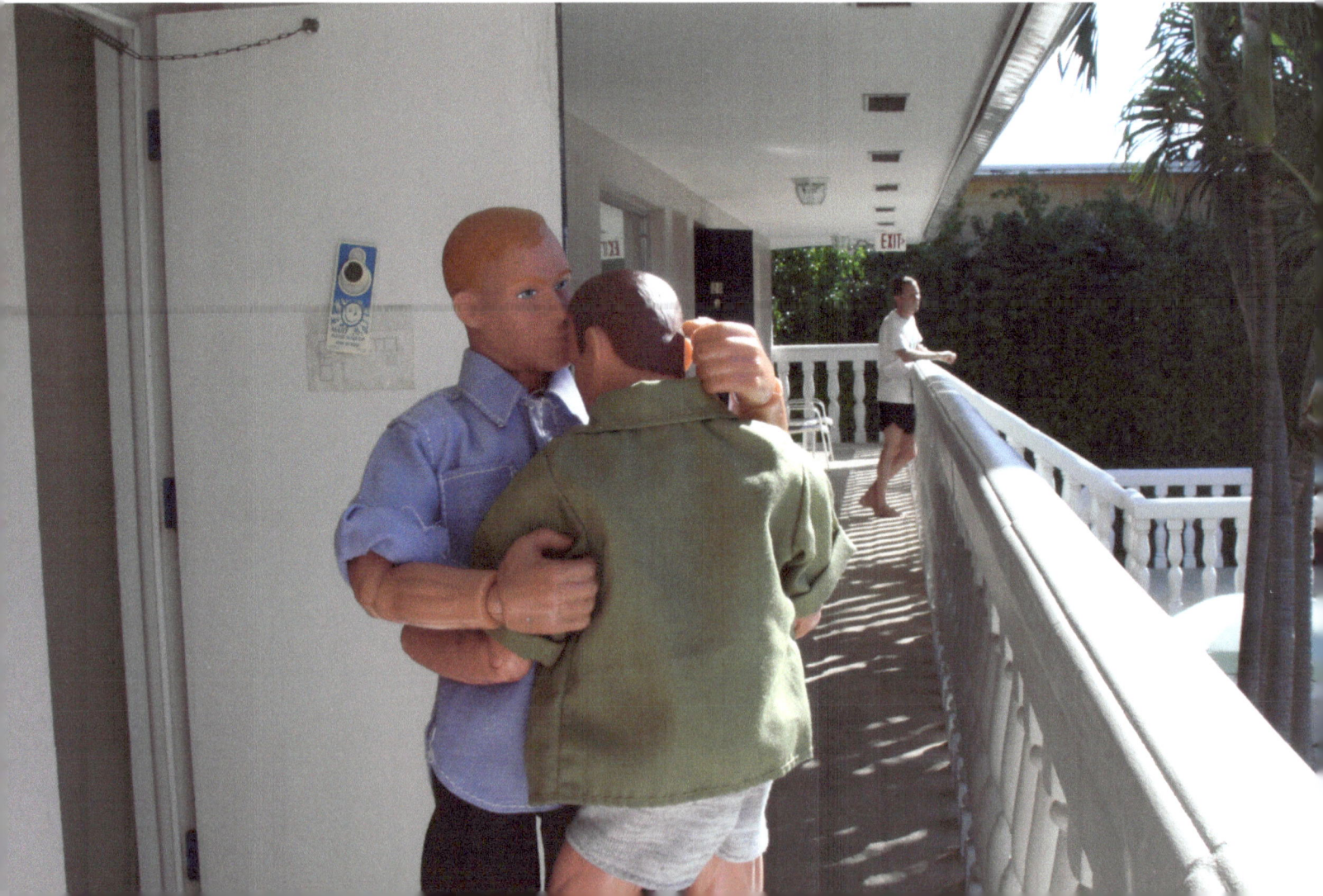

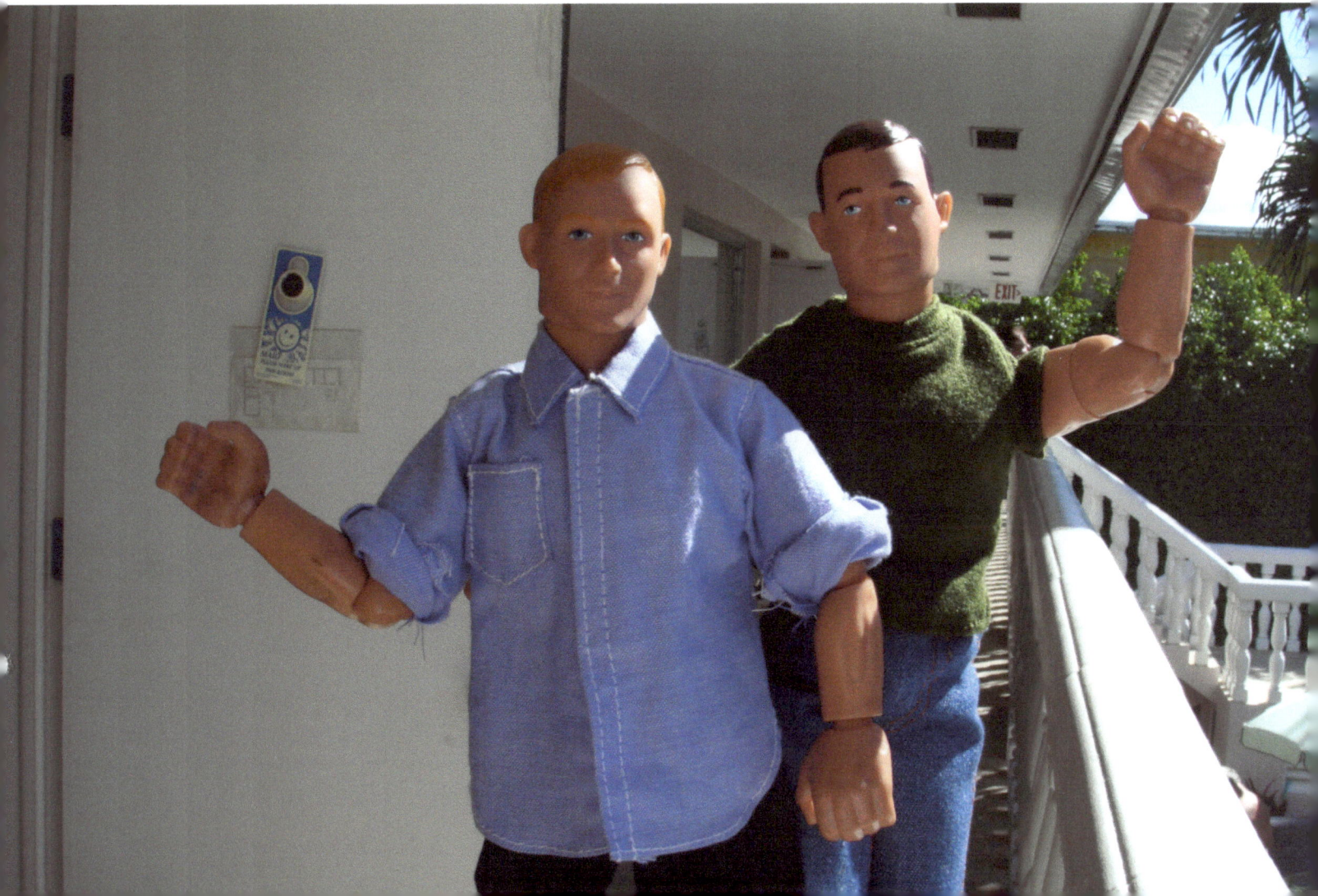

Rental Car
Return

Hotel

www.ingramcontent.com/pod-product-compliance
Lightning Source LLC
Chambersburg PA
CBHW041421290326
41932CB00042B/38